YOU CHOOSE

CAN YOU CREATE THE NORSE COSMOS?

An Interactive Mythological Adventure

by Gina Kammer

CAPSTONE PRESS
a capstone imprint

Published by Capstone Press, an imprint of Capstone.
1710 Roe Crest Drive, North Mankato, Minnesota 56003
capstonepub.com

Library of Congress Cataloging-in-Publication Data is available on the Library of Congress website.
ISBN 9781666337723 (library binding)
ISBN 9781666337730 (paperback)
ISBN 9781666337747 (ebook PDF)

Summary: You are the mighty god Odin. You dream of building new worlds and gaining great knowledge and wisdom. But realizing these dreams won't be easy. You'll need to face powerful giants and monsters and make great personal sacrifices. Will you find a way to overcome the obstacles to create the cosmos and truly become the All-father? It's up to YOU to choose how your story unfolds and if it leads to your glory—or your ultimate fate!

Editorial Credits
Editor: Aaron Sautter; Designer: Bobbie Nuytten; Media Researcher: Morgan Walters; Production Specialist: Polly Fisher

All internet sites appearing in back matter were available and accurate when this book was sent to press.

Printed and bound in China. 5995

Table of Contents

About Your Adventure

You are a god fated to die. You are the god of poetry, wisdom, and battle. You are the All-father, the one-eyed god—you are Odin. You often disguise yourself in a cloak and hat to travel among humans. Your two ravens land on your shoulders to bring you news. Nothing is hidden from you. But to gain your great knowledge, you will have to make great sacrifices. Can you survive the journey?

Chapter One sets the scene. Then you choose which path to take. Follow the directions at the bottom of each page. Your choices will determine what happens next. After you finish your path, go back and read the others for more adventures.

YOU CHOOSE the path you take through this mythical adventure!

According to Norse mythology, Ymir was the first giant and was the father of the race of giants.

Chapter 1

FIRE AND ICE

In the space between Muspelheim and Niflheim, the worlds of fire and ice, an enormous creature appears. It is Ymir, father of the giants, formed from the waters of Niflheim's melted ice. A huge cow also forms from the waters in the gap between worlds. It licks and licks the salty ice. Eventually, Buri, the father of the race of gods, is freed from the ice. Nothing else exists.

Ymir drinks the cow's milk and grows bigger and bigger. From Ymir's body, three giants are born. The god Buri marries one of the giants, and they have a son named Bor. Later, Bor marries Bestla, a giant woman, and they have three sons. You, Odin, are the oldest. Vili and Ve are your younger brothers.

Turn the page.

You are stuck in the emptiness between the worlds. Ymir continues to grow to immense size and becomes more and more cruel. To the south, you see the burning flames of Muspell across the vast space. The mists of Niflheim create a haze in the north. But here in Ginnungagap—the huge empty gap where you, Vili, and Ve grew up—there is nothing. No other worlds exist.

You've always craved more, and you long to escape. You thirst for knowledge, wisdom, and power. And you dream of a cosmos full of other worlds to explore. Perhaps you and your brothers can fill the emptiness and create such a cosmos. But the race of giants stands in your way. You'll need to make great sacrifices to fill the void.

To kill Ymir and create your own universe, turn to page 11.

To seek out wisdom, knowledge, and power, turn to page 39.

To learn the secret to gaining magic, turn to page 63.

Norse myths say that the giant Ymir grew to an unbelievable size by drinking milk from the cow Audhumla.

Chapter 2

The Worlds of Gods and Giants

You dream of having more . . . more knowledge, more power, and more worlds. Ymir is larger than the current worlds combined. You watch him lying on his back, drinking the milk of the cow, Audhumla. Meanwhile, you and your brothers have basically nothing.

Ymir is a being of evil and chaos. You turn to Vili and Ve to discuss the idea of killing Ymir. It would be nearly impossible. But it's the only way to turn that evil and chaos into a universe of order and life.

Turn the page.

You all agree to kill Ymir. But how? Ymir is enormous and powerful. You look at your options. The other frost-giants won't help. You don't really get along with them.

But there might be one possibility. With his flaming sword, Surt, the guardian of fiery Muspell, could certainly challenge Ymir. However, you know Surt never leaves Muspell. Should you try to battle Ymir on your own? Or should you get Surt to help?

To go to Surt and ask for his help, go to page 13.

To battle Ymir yourself, turn to page 17.

You realize that Muspell's guardian is a fire giant. Ymir was born from melting ice. Surt would be a better match for Ymir than you and your brothers. You tell Vili and Ve your plan. They're not so sure. None of you would survive traveling to fiery Muspell. But they agree that Surt has the better chance of beating Ymir. You know Surt is at the edge of Muspell. Perhaps you could at least get near enough to speak with him.

You near Muspell's heat. It's nearly unbearable, but you push on. You see Surt standing guard at the edge of his realm, holding his flaming sword before him. His flesh is charred black, and the flames rise high around him. Sparks spit out from the flames, crackling and popping in front of you. It's impossible to get any closer.

You call out loudly to Surt, asking for help. But he doesn't even notice you. He stares off into the distance.

Turn the page.

The fiery giant Surt guarded Muspelheim. He would play a key role in Ragnarök, the end of the world in Norse mythology.

You call louder, but he's still too far away. Lava bursts out of a crevice in front of you. You jump back just in time, but you think you see a way across. Do you risk getting closer? Or maybe it's best to give up on Surt and battle Ymir on your own after all.

To get closer to Surt and ask for help, go to page 15.

To give up and battle Ymir on your own, turn to page 17.

Surt continues to stare off into the distance. He won't even look in your direction. The roar of the flames might be too loud for him to hear you. But you're sure he must know you're there. He's the guardian of Muspell, after all. He surely knows when someone approaches his world.

You won't let Surt ignore you. You've come too far to give up now. You see a way across the lava and push on.

Vili and Ve scream at you, "Stop! It's too hot. Muspell only holds death for us."

You glance back to see if your brothers are following, but the rock you used to jump across has already melted. You wave them back instead. "It's all right! Go back. I'll go on alone."

The fires scorch your skin, but finally you get just close enough for your voice to reach Surt when you call.

Turn the page.

"Please!" you plead with him. "Aid us in our fight against Ymir."

Surt stares back at you with blank eyes. "It is not my destiny to leave Muspell until Ragnarök."

You drop your head. He will not help you.

The heat is becoming unbearable. You realize your mistake too late. Your wisdom was clouded by your selfish desires and pride. You know the flames and lava will soon overwhelm you, and you will not survive Muspell.

Your dying wish is that Vili and Ve make it back safely. You hope they can beat Ymir without Surt's help—or yours. But deep down, you know that's only wishful thinking.

THE END

To follow another path, turn to page 9.
To learn more about Odin and the Norse cosmos, turn to page 101.

Your first attack against Ymir does not go well. You gasp for air, gazing up at the huge giant. Your brothers stand beside you, panting and tired. They look at you, and you nod. It's time for one last charge. Vili leaps to crash his weapon against the giant's knee. As Ymir stumbles, Ve rushes in to strike a blow on Ymir's head.

Your brothers have given you a real opening. This is your chance—your last chance. With a cry, you charge and heave your spear at the giant's heart. Your weapon finds its mark, and then you pull the spear free. The other giants nearby call out in shock. They were not involved in the fight. They only watched.

As Ymir falls, his saltwater blood pours out in gushing rivers. You and your brothers scramble up onto the giant's body. The waters are so great and powerful that the sudden flood kills all the other giants. No one is left to stand in your way.

Turn the page.

Only one giant, Bergelmir, and his family escape the flood. They survive by floating on a box like an ark. But you don't want to bother with him right now. He's not an immediate threat to your plans.

Ymir's body is your prize. Now you and your brothers have something to use to make the worlds you've dreamed of creating. You grin at your brothers, and they cheer. You've won!

Together, you move Ymir's body to the center of the gap between worlds. You use the giant's flesh to make soil. His broken bones and teeth become mountains and rocks. From his hair, you create trees. And with Ymir's blood, you make the sea.

You soon find maggots in Ymir's flesh. You and your brothers discuss what to do with them.

"Let us give them intelligence," says Vili. Ve nods in agreement.

You take your time to decide what to do. You want to make sure that your choice is wise. It could be dangerous. You don't know how these creatures might use such knowledge. They might become your enemies.

To give the maggots intelligence, turn to page 20.

To leave the maggots alone, turn to page 34.

You agree with your brothers and decide to make the maggots more intelligent. After all, you are working to bring order to the cosmos. Together, you and your brothers give the creatures a shape and knowledge. These creatures become dwarfs.

Dwarfs were dark in appearance and lived underground in soil and rock.

You 're pleased with your work. The dwarfs will have an important role to play. You set up Ymir's giant skull over the earth with a strong dwarf at each corner. Together, they hold it up as the sky. These dwarfs are Nordri, Sudri, Austri, and Vestri. They represent the directions north, south, east, and west.

Using stray sparks from Muspell, you fix lights in the sky to become stars, planets, and comets. You then set them into motion, creating the days and years. Then with a great throw, you, Vili, and Ve toss Ymir's brains into the sky to make the clouds.

Thc world taking shape before you makes you and your brothers laugh with joy. It is so much more meaningful than the nothingness you lived in before. You look out at the flat, circular world you've created. The sea runs around the outer edge. Inside are meadows, forests, lakes, and mountains.

Turn the page.

But you almost forgot about the giants. You see some in the distance. They didn't all die in the flood of Ymir's blood. Bergelmir and his family escaped and continued the race of giants. You're wary of the chaos and destruction they could cause. Yet you know good can come from them too. After all, you yourself are descended from giants.

"What should we do with the giants?" Ve asks you.

"Let's give them the edges of the land closest to the sea," you reply.

"What will keep them from taking revenge on us for killing Ymir and the others in the flood?" Vili asks.

"Giants may attack our new world," Ve says, nodding in agreement.

You know your brothers are right. You come up with an idea to protect some of the world from the giants. You still have Ymir's eyelashes. You could create a fortress around the middle of the world to keep the giants out.

The only other option is to trust them to stay in their own lands. You've just created a whole world for them to explore. Perhaps you can come to an understanding with them.

To build a wall to keep the giants out,
turn to page 24.

To trust the giants to stay in their own land,
turn to page 32.

You consider your brothers' concerns. You agree that the giants could cause problems. You decide to build a wall to keep them out of the middle of the world.

"We'll make a wall to keep the giants out. We can use Ymir's eyelashes."

You explain your plan to your brothers. Slowly, Vili and Ve nod. They help you construct a fortress around the middle of the world. You name the land within it Midgard, or Earth.

You've created a beautiful world. But you know it isn't complete until it has people to live there. Searching across Midgard, you and your brothers find it empty. You look everywhere but find no one living among the vast landscapes. While walking along the sea, you find only a couple of logs on shore.

"Maybe we should split up," you say. "I'll go to the mountains while you two search the caves."

Your brothers shrug. You can tell they don't believe they'll find any people. You've all searched long and hard already. But there are still so many things you don't know about your new world. Just as the maggots had appeared on their own, perhaps other creatures will too. You don't yet know what's in the mountains.

Your brothers seem to have other plans. Vili stands one of the logs on its end and looks at it curiously. You wonder what your brothers are up to, but you don't want to waste any more time. You look back at the mountains, hazy in the distance. Should you continue on or stay?

To search for people in the mountains,
turn to page 26.

To stay and see what your brothers are doing,
turn to page 29.

You shake your head at Vili and Ve as they play with the logs. Your quest to find people for your world is important, and Vili and Ve are just wasting your time. They start to tell you something, but you head off on the long journey to the mountains before they finish speaking.

Days, then weeks, and then years pass. You've circled all around the mountains but found nothing but cold, craggy peaks and empty lands.

You return to the beach to look for your brothers. But Vili and Ve are long gone. You sense that they've left Midgard completely. You don't blame them. You were gone for a very long time.

Trudging along the shore, you spot two clothed figures ahead. They're just shadows against the sea mist. You run toward them through the sand, calling out. But they don't greet you in return.

When you get near, you see that the figures are just carved logs that look like people. There's no life in them. However, the figures' faces are very lifelike. They look as if they can actually see you and understand you. Their lips look ready to speak, but no breath comes from them.

You sigh. You now understand what Vili and Ve did with the logs after you left. They decided to stop searching for beings that didn't yet exist. They understood it was their job to create people.

Turn the page.

Your brothers probably realized the truth after you left. But without you, they could not give the people the breath of life.

Staring out over the water, you wonder if it's too late to bring the wooden figures to life. But deep down, you know that they needed the breath of life first.

Now Midgard is only populated with wooden people who can never live. You lost sight of the order you created. You tricked yourself into thinking you could find what you were looking for on your own. You were so blinded by your desires that you didn't see your real purpose. If only you had more knowledge!

THE END

To follow another path, turn to page 9.
To learn more about Odin and the Norse cosmos, turn to page 101.

You look back at Vili wrestling with the ash wood log. He's starting to get excited.

Ve picks up the elm log that was next to the other. He stands that one on its end too.

As you watch, you finally catch on. You move in to get a closer look. First, you hold the ash log and study it closely. You breathe on it to give it the breath of life. Then you do the same with the elm log. The logs are now alive.

Vili then gives them minds to think and the ability to move. But they are still shaped like logs. So Ve gives them human shapes. He gives the logs faces with eyes, ears, and lips so that they can see, hear, and speak.

You then give these first humans clothes and names. You name the first man Ask for the ash tree. The woman was made from the elm tree. You name her Embla.

Turn the page.

These are the first people in your new world. You give them Midgard to live in with their future children.

Happy and satisfied, you go on to make a home for yourself. You create Asgard where you, your children, and the other gods can live. Finally, you build a rainbow bridge, called the Bifrost, that connects Asgard and Midgard.

Sitting in Hlidskjalf, your throne in Asgard, you see everything you've created. You watch the humans, the gods, and all their doings.

You, the All-father, take it all in. You've achieved much. You've filled the nothingness of Ginnungagap as you had set out to do.

But even so, you can't help but crave more—more wisdom and more power. You know that nothing will stop you from achieving your desires.

After creating the cosmos, Odin watched over his creation from his home in Asgard.

THE END

To follow another path, turn to page 9.
To learn more about Odin and the Norse cosmos, turn to page 101.

The giants still pose a threat to your beautiful creation. They are too hostile. You nearly succeeded in wiping them out once before. You don't think they'll let that go very easily.

On the other hand, you created a world for the giants and their families to make their homes in. Surely you can come to an agreement. You meet with Bergelmir and explain that he should respect the worlds you've created.

"You must live in the areas we've given you," you explain. "The land in the middle, Midgard, will be for others."

Bergelmir seems wise. He listens to you and agrees, although his shoulders slump a little as he starts to leave. You thank him for his understanding and hope the rest of his kind will follow his lead. But as he glances back at you, you catch a fiery glint in his eyes. Still, he smiles and goes home.

As you return to your brothers, you try not to think about the uneasy feeling the giant's sly look gave you.

The next day, you discover the giants' true intentions. They've already overrun your world.

"We've lost Midgard!" shouts Ve.

"We can't push them back!" Vili says.

Your brothers are right. The only way to return the world to order from the giants' chaos is to destroy everything you've created. You can only add to their disorder.

"All is lost," you say, hanging your head. "Our order of the world is unbalanced. It is ruined."

You should have never trusted the giants.

THE END

To follow another path, turn to page 9.
To learn more about Odin and the Norse cosmos, turn to page 101.

You listen to your brothers' arguments, but something tells you it's better to refuse them. Without you, Vili and Ve can't give the maggots reason and intelligence of their own. You all have to work together.

You shake your head. "I'm sorry, brothers. I can't help you. These creatures could become too powerful. They could become evil."

"You will regret this!" Vili shouts.

You look around at what the three of you have created together. "There are others yet to bring to life. Wait and see."

Your brothers aren't happy, but they finally give in. Then you have an idea for creating a sky for your new world. You wave your brothers over to help you lift Ymir's great skull.

The three of you heave the skull over your heads. But your arms tremble under its weight.

Ancient Norse tales say that Odin used Ymir's immense skull to create the sky over the earth.

Turn the page.

"We cannot hold it!" Ve cries in alarm.

"Steady!" You caution him.

"How will we keep it in place?" Vili asks, gritting his teeth.

You look around, but you realize you weren't ready to create the sky at all. Nothing is in place to hold it up.

Your arms shake even harder. Soon, Ve buckles under the load. You can't carry it for him. And you know that your own strength is about to give out. As gods, the three of you can do great things. But you are not fated for the task of holding up the sky.

You see now that the maggots could have become strong dwarfs. Perhaps even strong enough to hold up the sky. You wish you would have had the wisdom to see it all earlier.

"I'm . . . sorry." You choke the words out just before the sky crushes you and your brothers beneath it.

THE END

To follow another path, turn to page 9.
To learn more about Odin and the Norse cosmos, turn to page 101.

Odin ruled over Asgard from his throne, called Hlidskjalf, with his wife, Frigg, by his side.

Chapter 3

THE EYE IN THE WELL

You refused to be trapped in the gap between worlds. Killing Ymir was your only option. You, Vili, and Ve fought him, and together, you won. Then you and your brothers created the rest of the cosmos from his enormous body.

You've achieved much. You've filled the nothingness as you had intended. And, although there is continual conflict with them, you're part of a family of gods now too, including the Aesir and the Vanir.

But, in spite of all you've achieved, you still crave more. Your throne allows you to see the worlds you've created.

Turn the page.

Yet seeing your creation isn't enough. You desire more wisdom, more knowledge, and more power over the cosmos.

Altogether, nine worlds surround the World Tree, Yggdrasil. Each world holds its own secrets, dangers, and wonders. You look out over them and see your uncle Mimir's well. It is the well of wisdom. You watch Mimir drink from it every morning using the special horn called Gjallarhorn. You lick your lips, wondering what a sip of that knowledge would taste like.

Peering across the cosmos, you see the giant Vafthruthnir in his hall. Your wife, Frigg, tells you no giant is wiser than he is. Though you are very wise, there is much you don't yet know. You tighten your knuckles on your throne. None should be wiser than you! You itch to pit your knowledge against Vafthruthnir's.

People in several ancient cultures often used hollow cow or goat horns to store and carry water or other drinks.

You lick your lips once more and look across the giant's land of Jotunheim to Mimir's well. You long to drink from the well, but you also must know whether the giant is wiser than you.

To seek knowledge from Mimir's well, turn to page 42.

To test your wisdom against the giant Vafthruthnir, turn to page 54.

You decide that Vafthruthnir can wait. You'll test your knowledge against his another day. The real prize is the knowledge you might gain from Mimir's well. The well feeds the roots of the World Tree, but it's in dangerous giant territory.

You swing your long gray cloak around your shoulders and fasten it shut. You also put on your broad-brimmed hat and pull it down to cover your face. Then you begin your journey. You pretend to be a wanderer, hoping no one stops you.

Thanks to your disguise, you arrive at the well without incident. You see Mimir standing beside the clear waters at the roots of the World Tree.

"Uncle!" you call to him. "Let me have one drink of the water of your well."

Mimir doesn't reply. He only shakes his head. Frustrated, you try again. "Mimir, you are my uncle. You are the brother of Bestla, my mother."

"That does not matter," Mimir says.

"I only ask for one drink so that I may gain knowledge and wisdom. What do you need from me?" you ask.

Mimir says, "You already risked your life to get here. But that isn't enough. You will need to pay a greater price."

You pause and think. What could Mimir want in addition to you risking your life?

"Tell me," you say, setting your jaw tightly. "What is the price?"

"Your eye," Mimir said. His face is serious. "I require your eye in the well."

You freeze. How can you possibly give your uncle your eye?

To refuse to give up your eye, turn to page 44.

To agree to sacrifice your eye, turn to page 46.

You can't possibly lose your eye. You refuse. "No, uncle. I cannot sacrifice my own eye. It is too great a price."

Your uncle shrugs. "That is the price."

"I came here for wisdom," you argue. "I need to see better, not worse! How can I see better and have greater wisdom with only one eye?"

Mimir stares at you intensely. You sense that he's trying to get you to understand something.

"What?" you ask, frustrated.

Mimir only shakes his head. "If you can't see it, then you are not worthy to drink these waters."

You growl. "See what?"

Mimir waves you away with his hand. "Go home to Asgard."

"Do you have any idea what I went through to get here?" You respond angrily. "I crossed

Jotunheim! I had to pretend to be a wanderer just so I wouldn't be killed."

Mimir speaks quietly. "I believe I do know."

"Then you know how much I risked to come here! Why won't you give me what I ask? Just one drink!" You can tell your arguments are getting you nowhere. But you must try.

"Leave," Mimir says simply, his tone has a sharp edge. You know he's serious, and he will allow no more arguing.

You shake your head, glaring at him. Finally, you turn and pull your hat down over your face. You just hope you can make it back through Jotunheim alive. This was a wasted trip, and you are no wiser.

THE END

To follow another path, turn to page 9.
To learn more about Odin and the Norse cosmos, turn to page 101.

The sacrifice is great, but your desire for wisdom is greater. You take a deep breath as you grab your knife. With one swift motion, you pluck out your eye and hold it in your hand. Then you carefully lower it to the well. The eye continues to stare upward as it sinks below the water.

Silently, Mimir hands you the Gjallarhorn. You dip it into the water of Mimir's well, filling it to the brim. You bring the horn carefully to your lips and drink the cool water. You tip back the horn until you swallow the last drop, closing your remaining eye.

You feel the waters flood you with their wisdom. You open your eye in shock. Suddenly, you can see far better and so much more than before—even though you have only one eye.

You will be called the blind god, but you see more than anyone knows. You go home, thankful

Though he had only one eye, Odin still kept watch over the cosmos with the help of his two ravens, Huginn and Muninn.

you were able to make the sacrifice for such great knowledge and wisdom. But you still don't know everything . . .

* * *

Years later, as you sit in Asgard, a messenger brings you a strange package. You open it to find Mimir's head! You stare at it in shock.

Turn the page.

The Aesir gods and the Vanir gods were constantly at war with one another. But they were tired of it. To end the conflict, the Aesir and Vanir each sent their best man to the other side. They traded chiefs, and Hoenir was made chief of the Vanir gods.

You and the Aesir gods sent Mimir to counsel Hoenir. He made wise decisions when Mimir helped him. But whenever Mimir was gone, Hoenir couldn't decide on anything.

Clearly, the Vanir gods got angry. But it was Mimir's head they cut off. They knew it would hurt you more to lose Mimir. They sent his head to you to make sure you got the message. They didn't think Hoenir was a fair trade.

How will you respond?

To remain calm and accept Mimir's head, go to page 49.

To take revenge for your uncle's death, turn to page 52.

You sigh. There was a time when you would seek revenge. But you have much more wisdom now. You know it's not worth getting angry. You might be the battle god, but the war between the Aesir and the Vanir had come to an end. You don't want to start up the war all over again.

But losing Mimir and his knowledge is still unfortunate. He always had good advice. However, you might have another plan.

You take your uncle's head and carefully prepare it. You rub special herbs over Mimir's head. As you work, you begin to chant. You hope the charm will work.

You chant louder and faster. Quickly, you apply more herbs. But nothing happens. You stay calm and keep up the spell. But soon you run out of herbs. You wonder if you should stop to get more, but then you notice movement.

Turn the page.

Mimir's head opens its eyes. Then he begins to speak. You smile. Mimir gives you good advice, as he always has. Even more, Mimir tells you things from other worlds! You decide to keep Mimir's head safe, and you know just the place for it.

* * *

The waters of Mimir's well were said to provide great wisdom and knowledge about the Norse universe.

Under the huge roots of the World Tree, you step up to the clear waters of Mimir's well. Your own eye stares back at you from its depths. You carefully set Mimir's head into the pool with your eye. Mimir will live on in the well, in a certain way. And you can still be counseled by his wisdom when needed.

You spot the Gjallarhorn beside the well. Picking it up, you study it. Without Mimir to drink from it and guard it, you think of a different god who can keep it safe. You tuck it inside your cloak, planning to give it to Heimdall. The guardian of Asgard will blow the horn to awake the gods when enemies approach at the end of the world.

THE END

To follow another path, turn to page 9.
To learn more about Odin and the Norse cosmos, turn to page 101.

When you look at Mimir's lifeless face, your rage builds. His great wisdom is lost. Never again will he be there to counsel you.

Thanks to Mimir's well, your greater wisdom tells you to pause before taking action. Like an itch in your mind, it keeps telling you to stop and think. But your anger becomes too great. You don't care if you aren't acting wisely—after all, the Vanir gods didn't! They were foolish to kill Mimir!

You are the war god, and you will show the Vanir gods just how foolish they were. You don't bother to bring an army of Aesir gods with you. Your power should be enough on its own. Your rage fuels you and gives you the power to destroy anything in your path.

But the Vanir gods are ready for you. They knew how you would react when they sent your uncle's head.

Even though you are the battle god, you aren't truly ready for battle at all. You didn't prepare. When the Vanir meet you in full armor and their weapons ready, you don't stand a chance.

A spear pierces you. A sword cuts through you. Suddenly, you are surrounded by enemies. Wait, these aren't truly your enemies. They're gods too! You shouldn't be fighting them, no matter how they angered you. But it's too late. You're dying, and you don't feel you're worthy of going to Valhalla—your own hall.

THE END

To follow another path, turn to page 9.
To learn more about Odin and the Norse cosmos, turn to page 101.

You can't stand the thought of a frost-giant being wiser than you. You decide you want to know just how wise you are before going to drink from Mimir's well.

You tell your wife, Frigg, your plans. "Go," she tells you. "But be safe and come home again!"

You nod to Frigg, and then quickly grab your cloak and hat to disguise yourself. You won't let the giants know who you are. It will be much safer that way.

Eventually you arrive at the hall of the giant Vafthruthnir. "Hail!" you call. "I have come to see if you are really as wise as I've heard."

"Who comes to my hall? If you come in, you may never leave again unless you prove yourself wiser than me!" Vafthruthnir's voice booms out.

"I am called Gagnrath," you tell him. "My journey here has been long."

"Come in, then," the giant says. "Take a seat in my hall. We'll see who is the wiser. The loser will lose his head." He grins at you slyly.

You don't let the price of the bet bother you. You take your seat and Vafthruthnir takes his. "Tell me, Gagnrath," the giant begins, "what is the name of the horse that brings the day each morning?"

"Skinfaxi," you answer. "The best of horses! His mane burns brightly."

Vafthruthnir nods. "And which horse brings the night?"

"Hrimfaxi brings the night. The foam that falls from his bit is where the dew comes from." You smile. You know the answers, but what does Vafthruthnir know?

"Tell me," you say, "how did the earth and sky come to be?"

Turn the page.

The giant answers easily. "The earth was made from the giant Ymir's flesh. The sky was created from his skull."

"Do you know where the day and night come from?" you ask.

"The god Delling is the father of the day. Norr created the night. The moon was made for men to tell the time."

On and on go your questions back and forth. You ask about who the first giants were and where the wind comes from. You ask about the fate of the gods. Vafthruthnir knows every answer.

You start to worry. Perhaps the giant is wiser than you! You must think of a harder question. What should it be?

To ask what you whispered to your son, go to page 57.

To ask about your doom, turn to page 59.

You decide to make your final question the trickiest one of all. You think back to a painful memory. Your son Baldur was killed due to a prank by the trickster god, Loki. Before you sent Baldur off on his burning funeral ship, you whispered something in his ear. But your words forever remain a secret. Only you and Baldur know what you said.

Vafthruthnir grins while he waits on you. He probably thinks he's won. "What is your question, Gagnrath?"

But you think you have your winning question. You pull yourself out of the memory and ask, "What did Odin whisper to his son before he burned on his funeral pyre?"

Vafthruthnir's smile drops. He blinks a few times. Then he squints at you, looking at you more closely. You pull your hat down a little further over your eyes, but Vafthruthnir's smile returns.

Turn the page.

He replies, "No man can say what you spoke so long ago in the ear of your son. Odin, I have told you of all the things of old and the fate of the gods. But you are the wiser, and I am doomed."

You win! Vafthruthnir is not wiser than you after all. However, you realize that you've only won a contest. You haven't gained any more wisdom for yourself. This victory doesn't satisfy you quite as much as you thought it would.

THE END

To follow another path, turn to page 9.
To learn more about Odin and the Norse cosmos, turn to page 101.

Your final question needs to be one that Vafthruthnir can't possibly know the answer to. The giant knew much about the fate of the gods. But would he know your own fate? Your curiosity gets the better of you. You decide to ask who will bring about your doom—Odin's doom.

"I'm waiting, Gagnrath," the giant says. "What is your question? Just ask one. You know you won't be able to think of any I don't know the answer to."

To his servants, Vafthruthnir orders, "Get the axe ready! Soon we will know which of us will lose his head."

You hesitate. Could you be wrong? What if he does know your fate? But you can't think of a harder question. You take a deep breath.

Turn the page.

"My final question is this: What will be the doom—the death—of Odin at the end of the world?" You hold your breath, hoping the giant does not know the answer.

Norse myths say that Odin will be killed by the great wolf Fenrir when they meet in the final battle of Ragnarök—the end of the world.

But a grin slowly spreads across Vafthruthnir's face. "The All-father shall meet his fate by the great wolf Fenrir. The beast will kill and swallow him. Afterward, the wolf's powerful jaws will be torn apart when Odin's son avenges him."

You listen as your ultimate fate is spelled out for you. Yet you also see Vafthruthnir's sharp axe prepared to take off your head. Is it possible for a god to die twice? Either way, it seems you are doomed. Possibly worse, you've lost this battle of wits.

THE END

To follow another path, turn to page 9.
To learn more about Odin and the Norse cosmos, turn to page 101.

Odin and his two brothers, Vili and Ve, worked together to defeat and kill the giant Ymir. They then used his body to create the Norse cosmos.

Chapter 4

Odin and the World Tree

You knew you were meant for more than your meager existence in Ginnungagap. The only way out of that existence was to kill Ymir. Afterward, you and your brothers created everything else from the giant's massive body.

You then created your home, Asgard, and your throne, Hlidskjalf, where you sit now. Your seat allows you to see everything that goes on across your creation.

But while you have unique sight and wisdom, you're still not satisfied. You crave more knowledge and control over what you've created.

Turn the page.

You watch as the women called norns carve something into the World Tree, Yggdrasil. You see that they are carving runes that direct the fates of all. But you cannot understand the runes or what they say. This greatly bothers you. You must find out what they mean. You doubt you'll understand the runes any better by going to the World Tree. Yet you hope to learn more by studying them closely.

However, just as you're about to go to the tree, something else catches your attention. The giant Suttung is moving the Mead of Poetry to his mountain. You've wanted the mead for a long time. The drink was brewed from the blood of the wisest god, Kvasir, and holds great power. Perhaps it even holds the power to understand the runes.

To try to get the Mead of Poetry from Suttung, go to page 65.

To go to the World Tree and study the runes, turn to page 70.

You wonder how Suttung got the mead. The drink would give anyone who tasted it the gift of poetry. You summon your two ravens, Huginn and Muninn, to you. They bring you news from all over the nine worlds.

The flapping of the ravens' wings soon echoes through your hall. You feel Huginn land on your shoulder. Muninn lands on the other. You feel their talons dig into your cloak.

"What news do you bring? How did Suttung get the Mead of Poetry?" you ask them.

Huginn clicks his beak near your ear. Then Muninn makes a low croak. You understand what they are telling you.

"The dwarfs killed the parents of the giant Suttung," Muninn says. "Then Suttung kidnapped the dwarfs. The dwarfs bargained for their lives, giving up the Mead of Poetry."

Turn the page.

Huginn adds, "Suttung took the mead and let the dwarfs live. Suttung then gave the Mead to his daughter, Gunnlod, to guard in the mountain Hnitbjorg."

You think about how to get the mead from the giant. The giants aren't friendly toward you, and you know Suttung is very stubborn. His brother Baugi, however, is not as stubborn. You wonder if Baugi would help you or if you should go straight to Suttung and his mountain.

But first, you grab a simple drill and a whetstone. The drill can be used to cut through stone, and the whetstone can sharpen blades. You have a feeling you're going to need these tools if you're going to get the mead.

To speak with Suttung in his hall,
go to page 67.

To seek Baugi's help to get the mead,
turn to page 78.

You decide it's better to go straight to the source and seek out Suttung himself. The giant may be stubborn, but you know how to stand your ground.

At the edge of the mountains, Suttung's large hall looms up before you. The mountain crags behind it are snowy and steep.

"Suttung! The god Odin calls on you!" Your voice booms toward the hall.

A huge giant steps out and squints at you. "Why should I care about a god?" Suttung asks.

"Because you have something that belongs to us." You wait, hoping Suttung has some honor.

Suttung grunts. "What I have is now mine by right."

Gritting your teeth, you try to remain calm. "Kvasir was one of ours. His blood should be with the gods."

Turn the page.

Suttung shrugs. "That's not my problem. You let it be taken from you. But the dwarfs killed my parents. The mead is my payment. It's mine now."

A growl threatens to burst out of you just as Suttung speaks again. "Leave, Odin. You have no right to be here." With that, Suttung ducks back into his hall, leaving you standing outside alone.

Anger boils inside you. You are the All-father, and you won't tolerate losing to this giant. You study the great mountain Hnitbjorg. Its steep sides and sharp rocks rise high into the sky ahead of you.

You feel the drill you brought with you in one pocket. In the other, you have the whetstone. The tools might be useful to gain the aid of Suttung's brother, Baugi. He might be able to convince Suttung to give you the mead.

Climbing up the steep mountain Hnitbjorg and entering Suttung's protected hall would be a difficult task for Odin.

But Suttung has proven to be very stubborn. You doubt he'll change his mind. Maybe you should go to the mountain and try to break in yourself to find the mead.

To try to break into the mountain, turn to page 73.

To go to Baugi's farm and ask for help, turn to page 78.

The great trunk, roots, and branches of Yggdrasil loom up before you, chalky white. The norns, Weird, Verdandi, and Skuld, use the water and mud from Weird's well to cover the tree in mud. The mud keeps the tree from rotting.

The water from the well is so holy that it turns everything it touches white. It even turns the birds that feed at the well white. You approach, alone, as you watch two swans swim in the water.

Suddenly, a furry tail zips past you and up the tree's trunk. You jump. But it is only Ratatosk, the squirrel. You see the squirrel scurry up through the branches. He stops near the wise eagle in the high branches. He's probably carrying an evil message from Nidhogg, the serpent under the tree's roots.

On the tree, you see some of the runes that the norns carved. You step closer, studying them. But as you move toward another side you see a stag named Dain. He gnaws through the mud to get to some of the tree's bark.

Three other stags, Dvalin, Duneyr, and Durathror, are close behind. You try to shoo them away. You don't want them to destroy the runes. Dvalin dares to nip at you. But you smack the stag lightly with your spear. Finally, they move farther off.

Turn the page.

You stab your spear into the ground and lean on it like a walking stick. You let your eyes travel over the strange markings carved into the World Tree. An hour passes. Then two. You study the runes closer. Taking a few steps back, you squint, trying to see all the runes at once.

Nothing works. You're no closer to understanding the runes. They will only reveal themselves to those who are worthy. You need to do more than stare at the runes. You must make yourself worthy. To do so, it will take more sacrifice.

To sacrifice one of the stags, turn to page 75.

To make yourself the sacrifice instead, turn to page 81.

The mountain Hnitbjorg is treacherous. You push against the wind and icy gusts. Climbing up onto sharp crags, you're completely alone. No one helps you on the long journey.

Finally, you come to a ledge where you can get better footing. You're not sure if this side of the mountain is near the cavern in which the mead is kept. But you need to start somewhere.

You pull out your drill and set it to the side of the mountain. You wish you had a strong giant to help you drill the hole. After several hours pass, you still haven't gotten very far. You needed Baugi's help. Without him, you don't even know if you're drilling in the right place.

A strong gust of wind almost blows you off your ledge. You grab onto your drill, which is lodged in the small hole you've made. You hope it doesn't slip. Thankfully, it holds as the wind wails.

Turn the page.

You eventually gain a better stance, and you can loosen your grip on the drill. But just as you do, a sheet of ice and snow slides toward you. Your hand slips off the drill, and the ice and snow tear it out of the hole.

You stare after the drill as it tumbles down the mountain. You slump over in defeat. Without the drill, it's impossible to get in and find the mead. You head back to Asgard, feeling your failure the whole way.

THE END

To follow another path, turn to page 9.
To learn more about Odin and the Norse cosmos, turn to page 101.

The stag Dain wanders back to where you're studying the figures carved in the great tree. You watch him out of the corner of your eye.

Dain and the other three stags have tormented Yggdrasil endlessly with their chewing. The tree suffers greatly—more than many realize. Surely one of the stags would make a worthy sacrifice.

A stag is an adult male deer. Stags in ancient mythology are often large, noble creatures with huge antlers.

Turn the page.

Your mind is made up. Silently, you pull your spear out of the ground. You shift your weight and bend your knees, getting ready to strike.

Dain begins to gnaw at the trunk of the World Tree. The stag doesn't seem to notice you. You heft your spear and then swiftly thrust it forward. Dain falls, and you pick up the stag's lifeless body.

Taking a length of rope, you tie the dead stag to the tree. You offer it up to Yggdrasil in exchange for knowledge of the runes.

You take a step back from your work, focusing intently on the runes. You try not to blink, and your vision gets a little cloudy from staring so hard. But no matter how long you wait, nothing happens.

Finally, you realize this sacrifice wasn't enough. But you don't have the courage to give any more. You once sacrificed an eye to gain your knowledge. And you've risked your life many times. You've given all you can. Worse, you've killed this beautiful creature for nothing.

With the weight of your failure, you untie Dain's body and bury the stag. Exhausted and covered in dirt, you return to Asgard. You never learn what secrets the runes hold.

THE END

To follow another path, turn to page 9.
To learn more about Odin and the Norse cosmos, turn to page 101.

Fields of grass stretch before you. Baugi's nine workers swing their scythes in the field, harvesting hay. You grin as you touch the whetstone in your pocket. It is the whetstone of the gods, and you have a plan for how to use it.

"Hello!" you call to the workers. "Why are you using such dull blades?"

The nine giants pause in their work to look at you. A few of them test the edges of their scythes and frown.

"Here," you say, "let me sharpen your scythes with my whetstone."

The giants shrug and bring you their scythes. You run the whetstone along the edges of the blades, sharpening them better than ever before. Then you give the giants back their scythes.

"Wow!" one giant exclaims, testing the edge and cutting himself.

The others are also impressed. "That's no ordinary whetstone," one says. "This will make our work so much faster. But our blades will grow dull again in time. What can I give you for it?"

One of the other giants gets angry. "Why should you have it? I'm a better worker. Sell it to me." The other giants begin to argue.

You shake your head and stop them. "Oh, it isn't for sale. But how about this? I'll let you play a game to win it from me. Stand close together here."

You show them, and the giants stand together, nearly touching each other. "Now, I'll toss the whetstone into the air, and whoever catches it can have it."

The giants agree. They wait eagerly for you to throw the whetstone. When you toss it into the air, the giants all jump up to reach it.

Turn the page.

But as they jump, they're cut to pieces by their extra-sharp scythes. Together, they fall in a heap before you. It looks like they all fought one another to the death.

Pleased with your trick, you take the whetstone back. Now it's time to get Baugi to help you. You can try to trick Baugi, too, by wearing your disguise. But he is a stubborn giant. It might work better to threaten him to help you instead.

To wear a disguise and offer to work for Baugi, turn to page 83.

To threaten Baugi and make him help you, turn to page 90.

Taking a length of rope, you tie yourself to Yggdrasil's branches. You try not to think too hard about what you're doing. Deep down, you worry that the sacrifice you're about to make will be too much for you. It could be your doom. But you keep moving before you can talk yourself out of what needs to be done.

You grasp your spear and yank it out of the dirt. Then you quickly flip the spear around and thrust it into your side. You let out your breath in a gasp, trying to bear the pain.

Now you know the truth. It's not the World Tree that needs the sacrifice. It's you. Into the wind, you shout, "I offer myself, Odin, to myself!"

Part of you must be sacrificed, just as you once sacrificed one of your eyes for wisdom. The old you, who cannot understand the runes, must be given up. It is the only way to learn the true mystery of the runes.

Turn the page.

The first night passes. Then another. And another. No one comes to feed you or help you. This is the way it must be. Five more nights pass, and still you stay tied to the World Tree.

You gaze at the runes until they burn into your mind. You lick your dry, cracked lips, wishing for a sip of water. The wound from your spear throbs in pain. Worse, the wind shrieks and gusts, blowing against you.

You are dying. Your vision fades. You're so cold that you barely feel the chill wind. Still you do not have the knowledge of the runes.

You begin to doubt yourself. Maybe you were wrong. There must be another way to get the runes to reveal themselves.

To give up and save yourself, turn to page 88.

To wait one more night, turn to page 98.

You pull your cloak over you and tug your hat down further over your face. Then you go to see Baugi.

"I am Bolverk, a traveler looking for a place to stay," you tell the giant.

"I can't help you right now. I have too much to do," Baugi says. "I don't know why, but my workers have all killed each other. Now I have no one to bring in the harvest before winter."

"That is unfortunate," you say sadly. "But what if you hire me? Let me do the work instead."

Baugi looks at you, uncertain. "You're no giant. How can you replace my nine workers?"

"I'll make you a deal," you say. "I'll prove that I can do the work of nine giants. If I can't, you don't have to pay me anything. If I can, I only ask for one taste of the Mead of Poetry."

Turn the page.

Baugi frowns. "The mead is my brother's, not mine. I can't give it to you."

"Hmm . . . But you could ask him for me. You are his brother. You can convince him to let me have a small taste." You watch Baugi carefully.

"It's no use," Baugi says.

"All right. I'll just go, then." You start to walk away. "Good luck with your harvest!" You wave, hiding a sly smile.

"Wait!" Baugi calls. "I'll do it. If you can do the work and bring in my harvest, I'll ask my brother for some of the mead."

* * *

As Bolverk, you work harder than twenty men and impress Baugi.

"You deserve that mead!" Baugi says, clapping you on the back. "Let's go see my brother."

In many Norse myths, Odin is described as a mysterious traveler wearing a cloak and a wide-brimmed hat to cover his face.

Together, you go to Suttung's large hall at the edge of the mountains. Baugi tells Suttung your story. "So let my friend Bolverk taste the mead so I can keep my word."

Suttung stares at you both and says only one word. "No." Then he goes back to his hall, closing the door behind him.

Turn the page.

Baugi grows both angry and sad. "Not even for his own brother!" Baugi yells. "They were my parents too. I should also get some of the mead in payment!"

But it's no use. Suttung doesn't come back.

"Hey," you say. "Let's play a trick on him. Then your brother won't dismiss you like that ever again!"

Baugi smiles a little. He agrees.

You make the tough climb up the mountain Hnitbjorg together. Suddenly, you hear something through the sharp, cold wind. You put out your hand to make Baugi stop.

"It's Suttung's daughter, Gunnlod, singing," Baugi explains.

You nod. "Then this is where we stop."

You hand Baugi your drill to cut a hole into the mountain. He uses his great strength to twist the point into the stone. He pushes and twists again and again.

After a few minutes, he stops. "It's through," he tells you.

You blow in the hole, but dust blows back in your face. You eye Baugi suspiciously.

"Not yet," you say.

Baugi doesn't answer. He just starts drilling again. A few minutes later, he stops.

"Finished," Baugi says.

This time, you believe him. But you're not sure if you trust him. A giant is a handy ally, but maybe you should leave him behind.

To leave Baugi behind, turn to page 89.

To trust Baugi and continue on, turn to page 97.

The shrieking wind blows you yet again into the trunk of Yggdrasil. You can take no more. You grasp your spear with your numb hands and yank it out of your side. Using the spear's point, you cut the rope.

You don't have the strength to hold on to the rope, so you let yourself fall from the tree. Relief washes over you as feeling returns to your limbs.

Binding your spear wound, you pick yourself back up. You take one more look at the runes carved into the World Tree. The carved figures stare back at you. They seem to mock you as you try so hard to understand their meaning.

You sigh. You have lost so much and yet gained nothing in your failure.

THE END

To follow another path, turn to page 9.
To learn more about Odin and the Norse cosmos, turn to page 101.

You test the hole again. This time no dust comes back out. The drill has broken through.

But you sense something behind you. In an instant, you use your powers to turn yourself into a snake. As you do, you see Baugi slamming the drill into the side of the mountain—right where you'd just been standing! He must have been working for his brother the whole time!

As a snake, you're able to slip through the drilled hole before Baugi can catch you. You leave him behind on the side of the mountain.

Once in the large cave, you transform again. But this time, you pick the form of a giant. You're just in time to see Gunnlod, a giant woman, come into the chamber. Her eyes open wide when she sees you. Should you try to fight her, or pretend to be a friend?

To battle Gunnlod, turn to page 92.

To be friendly toward Gunnlod, turn to page 94.

"Baugi!" you shout outside the giant's home. "Your workers are dead. Your harvest is lost."

When Baugi comes out, he sees both you and his dead workers. "Odin. You did this!"

You smile. "You have no choice but to help me. You'll get your brother to give me the Mead of Poetry."

Giants are often the biggest rivals to the gods in Norse myths.

"Why would I help you?" Baugi asks angrily.

"Because I will save your harvest if you do," you reply.

Baugi glares at you. "No."

"Then I'll do it on my own," you shout at him. "Good luck with your harvest. It's too late to find new workers. Winter is coming."

"Leave! Now!" Baugi roars at you. "You don't scare me. Without me, you'll never be able to break into my brother's mountain. You'll never get the Mead of Poetry."

You let out a growl, but you turn to leave. You know that Baugi is right. You guessed wrong, and your plan failed.

THE END

To follow another path, turn to page 9.
To learn more about Odin and the Norse cosmos, turn to page 101.

Gunnlod glares at you. You dash to one side, but she's faster. The giant woman reaches out to grab you. You're not used to having a giant's body, and you trip trying to get away.

Gunnlod takes the opportunity to attack. She jumps on you and holds you down. "Who are you?" she demands.

"Bolverk," you gasp, as she presses your face into the cave floor.

"I am the guardian here. No one gets past me!" Gunnlod says, as she pushes you harder into the rock.

"Well, you haven't beaten me yet!" you say. You gather your strength and fling the giant woman off you.

Gunnlod falls back while you jump up and run. You can hear Gunnlod running close behind you.

Peering through the dark, you can't tell if there's a door ahead of you. You slow down and put out your hands. But you're too late. You run smack into a wall. You've hit a dead end.

Quickly, you turn around to take a fighting stance. Gunnlod slides to a stop in front of you. She looks fierce. You hesitate, not sure what to do. But soon it doesn't matter.

"What's going on here?" You hear a giant's voice boom through the caverns. It's Suttung.

"Father!" Gunnlod shouts. "Over here! There's an intruder!"

Oh, no—you've been cornered by two giants. There's no way out, and you can't win this fight with the odds against you.

THE END

To follow another path, turn to page 9.
To learn more about Odin and the Norse cosmos, turn to page 101.

"Who are you? How did you get in here?" Gunnlod asks, blocking your path.

"Bolverk is my name," you tell her, thinking fast. "Please don't worry. I'm only here to see your beauty."

Gunnlod stares at you in surprise.

"If only I could sing of your beauty. But I do not have the ability." You hang your head.

Gunnlod steps up to you cautiously. You look up and stare into her eyes. She is truly beautiful, so you hope your plan works.

"Let me take a small sip of the Mead of Poetry—one from each vat. Just enough to sing songs and create poems worthy of your beauty." You smile at her.

She breaks her gaze away from yours. "I don't know . . . my father wouldn't like that."

"He will never even know."

"I don't know if I can trust you," Gunnlod says, but she smiles as she speaks.

You're certain you've already convinced her, so you try a third time. "Gunnlod, your beauty is too great for my words. Let me try the mead so that I might have the right words."

Gunnlod's smile is bigger now. "All right then. But you must only take three sips. They must be so small that my father will never know."

"I promise," you say. Then you follow Gunnlod down a hall through the caverns to a room with three large vats of the mead.

Gunnlod keeps glancing behind her, but you don't hear anything. You drink from one of the vats so deeply that you drain it all. Then you drain the second and third!

Turn the page.

"You liar!" Gunnlod shouts at you. "You tricked me!"

Then she leaps forward to attack. Full of the Mead of Poetry, you change into an eagle just as Suttung comes running at Gunnlod's shouts. You flap your large wings and fly out through a secret door in the mountain. Suttung and Gunnlod shout angrily after you as you soar away through the sky.

Back in Asgard, you spit out the mead into new vats. From these, you will give it out to others as you see fit. You realize it won't help you understand the runes in Yggdrasil. But you've gained much wisdom and the gift of poetry.

THE END

To follow another path, turn to page 9.
To learn more about Odin and the Norse cosmos, turn to page 101.

You test the hole, and no dust comes back out. It has broken through into a cave.

"Yes," you say. "We're through this time."

But Baugi doesn't answer you. Suddenly, you sense something behind you. As you turn, you see Baugi with the drill raised to strike at you.

You cry out. "Baugi! What are you doing?"

"I'm sorry," Baugi says. "But if I stop you from stealing the mead, my brother might think better of me."

Your eyes dart all around, but there's no escape. When Baugi strikes, you quickly duck, and he misses. But then your foot slips, and you fall to the snow and jagged rocks far below. Your quest to get the mead is at an end.

THE END

To follow another path, turn to page 9.
To learn more about Odin and the Norse cosmos, turn to page 101.

You grit your teeth. No—you won't give up now. You must be close.

Holding out through one more day and night, you feel the last of your strength fade. Even so, you look down at the runes again. You concentrate on them as you prepare yourself to die.

Suddenly, the runes seem to come into sharp focus. They burn into your mind and sight. Finally, you understand the fates, things of other worlds, and their pure power—magic.

The runes carved in the World Tree contained the power and knowledge of magic.

But you are so weak. It is all too much at once. You cry out louder than the shrieking wind. The rope breaks, dropping you from Yggdrasil.

Though in great pain, you are too overjoyed to care. You finally understand magic. And you have the control over your creation that you so desperately desired.

Gaining back your strength, you read the runes carved on the tree. You learn word after word. You can feel your knowledge and wisdom growing greatly.

You grin as you pick up your spear and travel back to Asgard. There is so much more that you can do now that you've achieved your deepest desire.

THE END

To follow another path, turn to page 9.
To learn more about Odin and the Norse cosmos, turn to page 101.

The vast giant Ymir was the first creature to appear in Norse mythology. The tales say he was created from the melted waters of the icy world of Niflheim.

Chapter 5
CREATING THE COSMOS

According to Norse myths, the god Odin and his brothers, Vili and Ve, lived in a great void where nothing existed. Odin greatly desired greater knowledge, and he wanted to create worlds of his own. But he first needed materials for his creation. He saw that killing the vast giant Ymir would provide what he needed to achieve his goals. So he and his brothers battled Ymir and won. Using Ymir's body, they created the worlds of the Norse cosmos.

Odin created Midgard, also called Earth, around the trunk of Yggdrasil, the World Tree. It was a massive tree that connected all the worlds in Norse mythology.

From two logs, Odin and his brothers created the first humans, called Embla and Ask, to live in Midgard. Odin protected them from the giants by giving the giants their own land called Jotunheim. He separated this land from Midgard with a wall made from Ymir's eyelashes. Other races, such as dwarfs and elves, were formed and lived in their own worlds too.

From his throne in Asgard, the world of the gods, Odin could see all of his creation. Even so, he still craved more knowledge and power.

Odin gouged out his eye as the price for drinking from his uncle Mimir's well. The well's waters granted Odin great wisdom.

He also wanted to read and understand the runes carved into the World Tree. The runes were the language of the norns, or women who controlled fate. To do so, he had to sacrifice himself in a dangerous ritual to become worthy.

Asgard was said to be high in the upper branches of the World Tree so the gods could watch over all of creation.

Odin pierced himself with his spear and hung from Yggdrasil for nine days and nights. Finally, near death, he could understand the runes and gained the powers of magic. He could change shape and use spells.

Yet this still wasn't enough for Odin. He wanted to learn how wise and knowledgeable he truly was. In disguise, he tested his great knowledge on the wise giant Vafthruthnir in a battle of wits. The loser would lose his head. They each quizzed the other until Vafthruthnir could not answer Odin's final question. Odin proved his greater knowledge and won the contest.

But even this didn't satisfy Odin. He also desired the wisdom and inspiration of poetry. Dwarfs created the Mead of Poetry from a slain god's blood. Odin desired the mead, but a giant had stolen it.

Through tricks, shape shifting, magic, and his wits, Odin broke into the giant's stronghold and drank all three vats of the mead. After escaping back to Asgard, Odin spat most of the mead into new vats. From there he gave the gift of poetry to those he wished.

Through his adventures and cunning, Odin achieved great knowledge, wisdom, and power. His actions were done at first to fulfill his own desires. But he went on to share his gifts with others across his cosmos to become the All-father of Norse mythology.

More About NORSE MYTHS

Yggdrasil, the World Tree

Ancient sources describe few details about Yggdrasil. The home of the gods, Asgard, was located high up in the branches. Earth, or Midgard, was home to human beings. It was located around the tree's trunk. The other worlds were connected to the tree's roots and branches.

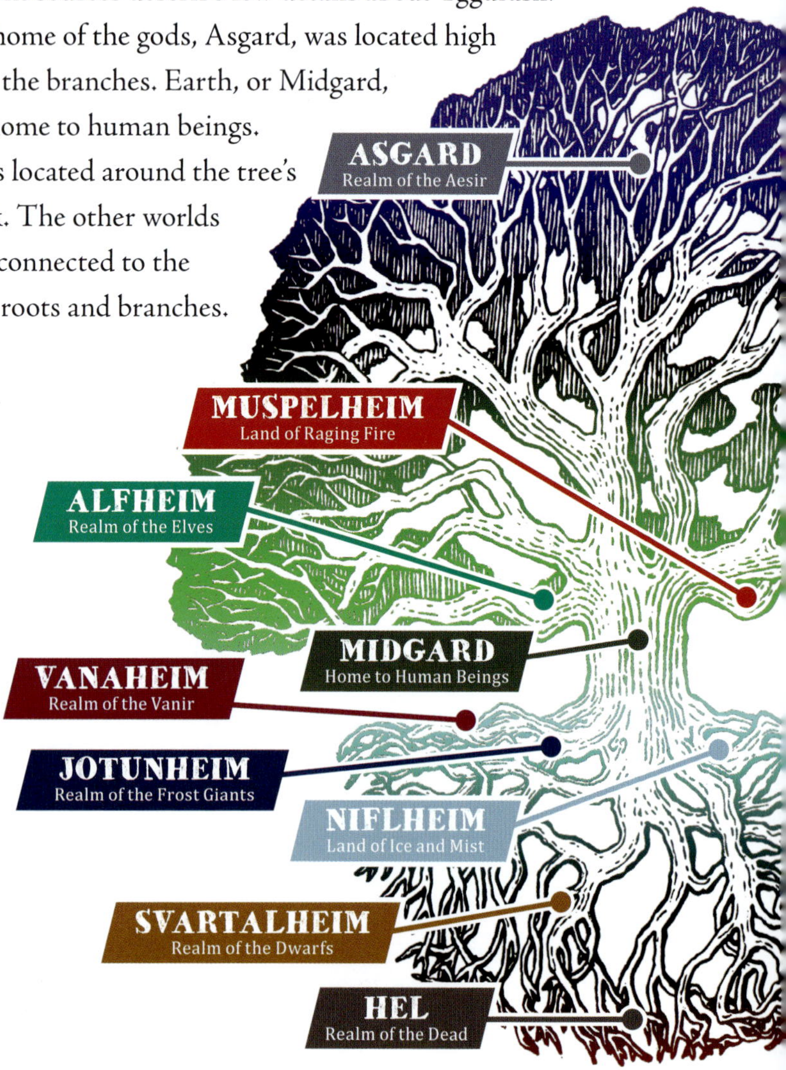

The Figures of Norse Mythology

Baugi (BOW-gee): a giant and a farmer; he was the brother of Suttung.

Bergelmir (bear-gel-MEER): the grandchild of Ymir, and the only giant (with his family) to survive Ymir's death

Gunnlod (GOON-lahd): the daughter of the giant Suttung; she guarded the Mead of Poetry.

Ginnungagap (JIN-noon-gah-gahp): the empty void between the worlds of ice and fire that existed before Odin created the cosmos

Hlidskjalf (LEED-skahlf): Odin's throne in Asgard

Hnitbjorg (neet-BYORG): the tall, steep mountain that was home to Suttung's hall

Mimir (ME-meer): a giant who guards a well with waters that grant wisdom; Mimir was Odin's uncle.

Odin (OH-din): the ruler of the gods, the creator of the Norse cosmos, and the All-father

Suttung (soo-TUNG): a giant and brother of Baugi; Suttung kept the Mead of Poetry inside his mountain.

Surt (SURT): a giant who guards Muspell, the world of fire

Vafthruthnir (VAHF-throoth-nihr): the wisest giant; Odin defeated him in a test of knowledge and wisdom.

Vili and Ve (VILL-ee and VAY): sons of Bor and Bestla, Odin's younger brothers

Yggdrasil (IG-drah-sihl): the World Tree that connected all the worlds of the Norse cosmos

Ymir (EE-mir): the first frost giant; his body was used to create the worlds of the Norse cosmos.

Other Paths to Explore

- Odin has several spiritual and animal helpers in Norse mythology. Huginn and Muninn are Odin's ravens. Their names mean "thought" and "memory." They bring Odin news and knowledge from across his creation. Odin also had wolves named Geri and Freki, and an eight-legged horse named Sleipnir. How might these helpers have aided Odin in his quest for knowledge and power?

- In many Norse myths, women were usually the ones given the gifts of prophecy and magic. But Odin sought wisdom and knowledge in every way he could. Why do you think he was so concerned with knowing the fates? Do you think he was seeking a way to change his fate?

- When the Aesir and Vanir gods grew tired of warring with each other, they came to a truce. They all spat into a vat to seal the deal. From their spit a new god was made named Kvasir, who had great wisdom. But one day, Kvasir traveled to Midgard and met two dwarfs named Fjalar and Galar. They led Kvasir deep into their fortress where they killed him and turned his blood into mead. This mead gave anyone who tasted it the gift of poetry. How might Odin's story be different if Kvasir had not been killed by the dwarfs?

Bibliography

Anderson, Rasmus B., trans. *The Younger Edda*. Reprint of the 1901 Chicago edition, Project Gutenberg, 2006. https://www.gutenberg.org/files/18947/18947-h/18947-h.htm

Ashliman, D. L. "The Norse Creation Myth." Folklore and Mythology Electronic Texts. University of Pittsburgh, February 17, 2010. https://sites.pitt.edu/~dash/creation.html.

Bellows, Henry Adams, trans. *The Poetic Edda*. Reprint of the 1936 Princeton edition, Internet Sacred Text Archive. John Bruno Hare, 2001. https://www.sacred-texts.com/neu/poe/index.htm.

Brodeur, Arthur Gilchrist, trans. *The Prose Edda*. New York: American-Scandinavian Foundation, 1916.

Byock, Jesse L., trans. *The Saga of the Volsungs: The Norse Epic of Sigurd the Dragon Slayer*. Berkeley: University of California Press, 1990.

Gaiman, Neil. *Norse Mythology*. 1st ed. New York: W. W. Norton & Company, 2017.

Hopkins, Joseph, J. H. Roberts, Ross Downing, Lauren E. Fountain, and Arjuna Thomassen. "Mimisbrunnr.info: Developments in Ancient Germanic Studies." Mimisbrunnr.info: Developments in Ancient Germanic Studies, December 1, 2021. https://www.mimisbrunnr.info/.

McCoy, Daniel. "The Ultimate Online Guide to Norse Mythology and Religion." Norse Mythology for Smart People, February 8, 2019. https://norse-mythology.org/.

Sturluson, Snorri. *Edda*. Translated by Anthony Faulkes. Viking Society for Northern Research. London: J. M. Dent, 2002. http://vsnrweb-publications.org.uk/.

Glossary

chaos (KAY-ahs)—a state in which behavior and events are not controlled by anything; the universe without order

fate (FAYT)—the things that will happen in the future; a controlling power

mead (MEED)—a wine-like drink made from water, honey, and yeast

populate (PAH-pyuh-layt)—to live in a place

rune (ROON)—a symbol in the alphabet of ancient Northern Europe

sacrifice (SAK-rih-fyse)—to give something up, including life, to get something else

scythe (SYTH)—a curved blade on a long handle for cutting crops

suspicious (suh-SPIH-shuhs)—in a manner that feels wrong or dishonest

whetstone (WET-stone)—a stone used for sharpening blades

Read More

Alexander, Heather. *A Child's Introduction to Norse Mythology: Odin, Thor, Loki, and Other Viking Gods, Goddesses, Giants, and Monsters*. New York: Black Dog & Leventhal Publishers, 2018.

Braun, Eric. *Odin*. Mankato, Minn.: Black Rabbit Books, 2018.

Crossley-Holland, Kevin. *Norse Myths: Tales of Odin, Thor, and Loki*. Somerville, Mass.: Candlewick Press, 2017.

Ralphs, Matt. *Norse Myths*. New York: DK Publishing, 2021.

Internet Sites

Children of Odin: A Collection of Norse Mythology
dltk-kids.com/world/norway/children-of-odin/index.htm

Norse Mythology Facts for Kids
kids.kiddle.co/Norse_mythology

Odin
norse-mythology.org/gods-and-creatures/the-aesir-gods-and-goddesses/odin/

The Vikings: Gods and Myths
vikings.mrdonn.org/gods.html

About the Author

Photo by Karon Dubke, Capstone.

Gina Kammer never grew out of Narnia and Middle-earth. Instead, she went on to study their medieval source texts, mythology, theater, and other literature at Bethany Lutheran College, Richmond University in London, and finally the University of South Dakota for her M.A. degree. Now she's an author, editor, and book coach specializing in science fiction and fantasy. She also occasionally teaches writing courses. Her other interests include tea, traveling, oil painting, archery, and snuggling her grumpy bunny. She lives among piles of books in Minnesota with her husband, daughter, and menagerie of critters. Find her at ginakammer.com.

Photo Credits
Alamy: AF Fotografie, 85, Ivy Close Images, 6; Getty Images: Filograph, 26, Michael Nicholson, 38, Sirozha, 41; Shutterstock: Bourbon-88, (ornament) Cover, DanieleGay, 62, 98, eleathyra, (mountains) design element, Cover, estevez, 69, grop, 106, Hanna Gottschalk, 75, HelloRF Zcool, 70, iobard, 100, Kalleeck, 47, Liliya Butenko, 10, Liu zishan, 31, Miki Pavlovikj, 90, NASA images, (space) Cover, top 8-9, NextMarsMedia, 103, Peter Litvik, 20, Stephani Elizabeth, 50, Thomas du Crest, 59, Tithi Luadthong, 1, 14, 35